This book belongs to:

Blake

This book is dedicated to my five grandsons, Mattox, Nolan, Sam, Graham and Eli who inspired me to write this book.

Special thanks to my husband and children for their support and especially my mom who made it all possible.

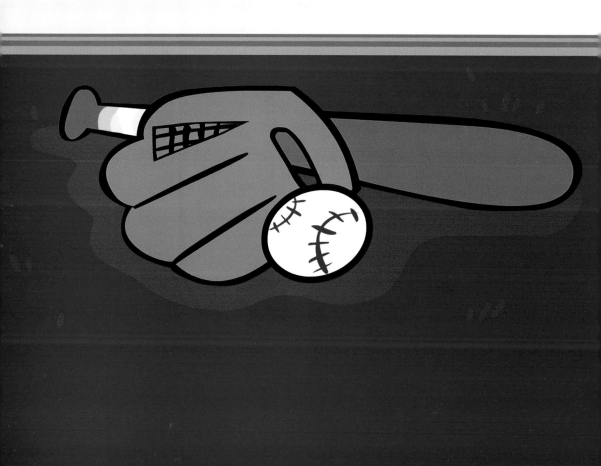

BASEBALL
The Best Game of All
By: Sissy Mattox
Illustrations: Amy Baniecki

Today is the day, that I get to play
the best game of all, the game of baseball.

I put on my uniform, I'm number eight.
I put on my hat and make sure it's on straight.

I put cleats on my feet,
grab my bat and my glove.
Now I'm off to play this
great game that I love!

To practice, we run, hit and throw.
Now we are all warmed up, and ready to go.

They play the "Star-Spangled Banner."
I put my hand on my heart.
After the song, the game is ready to start.

My position is pitcher so I run to the mound.
What a great inning: three up and three down.

It's my turn to bat. I want a hit really bad.
Instead I strike out but I don't get mad.

Now it's the bottom of the ninth inning.
My team has two outs and no one is winning.

It's my turn to bat and I really must try,
I don't want this game to end in a tie!

The next ball comes in a little bit low.
Trying to be patient, I just let it go.

The next pitch whizzes in fast, but way too high.
Again I don't swing--I let it go by.

The last pitch arrives.
I get one more try.
I hit the ball hard
and watch it fly.

Right down the middle and into the sun,
It sails over the fence...I've hit a home run!

I lay down the bat and circle the bases.
I hear cheers from my teammates
and see the smiles on their faces.

The other team came up a little bit short.
But it's always important to be a good sport.

So we form a line and as we walk by,
We shake their hands and tell them "Good try!"

At the end of the day, each of us is a winner...
We get to have popcorn and hot dogs for dinner.

Tonight when I sleep I will have just one dream, I'm the starting pitcher for my favorite Major League Team.